Life Perspectives

OTHER BOOKS BY PATRICIA CRUZAN

YOUNG ADULT & ADULT POETRY

Poetic Moments

My Reflections

Sketches of Life

MIDDLE GRADE FICTION

Henry the Sleuth

A Researcher or a Sleuth

What Anna Discovers

The Wonder in the Woods

FICTION FOR GRADES 1-3

Max Does It Again

Molly's Mischievous Dog

Tall Tales of the United States

Life Perspectives

Patricia Cruzan

Clear Creek Publishers
Fayetteville, Georgia

Published by Clear Creek Publishers
Fayetteville, Georgia 30215

Printed in the United States of America

Contents

Travels

A Restaurant Customer 1
Illinois's Storms 2
The Topography of the East 3
Traveling to New York 4
The River Thames 5
The Visitors of the Thames 5
Westminster Abbey 6
A Dome's Glory 7
The Eiffel Tower 8
Music and the Sidney Opera House 9
Mexico Recollections 10
The Virginia Landscape 11
Travel Suggestions 12
The Drive to Emory Clinic 13
Traveling in Town 14
A Mountain Trip 15

God and People

Hope for the Future 16
God Offers Hope 17
Calvary's Redemption 18
Death Long Ago on a Cross 19
What Life Might Be Like 20
A Package Mailed 21
Neighbors Behind Closed Doors 22
My Cousin 24
Mrs. Patel Finds Comfort 25
A Supper with My Brother 27

Kind Acts for a Special Loved One   28
A Homemade Quilt   29
Grandma's Cooking and the Cookie Jar   30
My Family as an Adult   31
Eating with Family   32
The Gift of Friends   33
The Reunion   34
Valiant People   35
The Internet's Pros and Cons   36
The Coronavirus   37
The Sun's Out   38
The Past Election   39
Not Considering Things Fast Enough   40
Obstacles to Being Blind or Partially Deaf 41
Living with Criticism   42

Animals

A Nature Walk   43
A Farm Visit   43
Deer Habits   44
The Wild Turkeys   45
A Rabbit Seeks Flora   46
Birds and Mates   47
Feathered Friends Seek Lunch   47
The Porch's Bird Nest   48
The Swooping Owl   49
Bernie, the Dog   50
A Cornered Hedgehog   51
An Unusual Rescue   52
The Cat's Hideouts   53

Color Poems

The Brightness of Orange   54
The Effect of Colors   54
How Colors Affect People   55
Gardening   56
White Objects   56
The Color Blue   57
The Color Gray   58
Red Gets Your Attention   58
Seeing the Color Brown   59
Black Items   60
Yellow Brightens the Day   61

Seasons and Holidays

Fall Arrives   62
Pumpkins and Costumes for Halloween   63
An Orange-Yellow Fruit   63
Thanksgiving Memories   64
Blessings for Thanksgiving   65
Winter Arrives   66
An Icy Blast   67
Christmas Is Upon Us   68
Decorating the Christmas Tree   69
Christmas Wrappings   70
Christmas Nights   70
Gifts for Writers   71
Ornaments or Jewels   72
A New Year   73
Groundhog Day   74
Valentines in February   75
Young Love   76

March Beginnings 77

A Breath of Spring 78

Is Spring Finally Here? 79

Spring Is Around the Corner 80

Appealing Blooms 80

Spring: A Time of Changes 81

A Mother Celebrated 82

Fathers' Qualities 83

Summers of the Young 84

Activities for the Summer 85

Vendor Fairs, Festivals, and Writing

The Fair at a Church 86

A Festival with Many Vendors 87

A Book Festival 88

Authors at the Decatur Book Festival 89

Budgeting Time 90

Finding Time to Write 91

Creating a Poetry Book 92

Spectators at a Fair 93

Senses and Emotions

Using Our Eyes 94

Ice Cream Treats 95

The Usefulness of House Rooms 96

The Chair 97

Little Things Mean a Lot 98

Thoughts Through Art 99

A Person's Emotions Alter 100

The ENT Visit 101

The Wait 102

The Unexpected News 103
Our Country's Flag and Freedoms 104
The Appeal of the Sea 105
Outside Sights and Sounds 106
The Brave Helping Others 107
Considerate Deeds 108
Happiness for Others 109
Different Food at Mealtime 110
Words Heard 111
Misapplication of Patience 112
Pluses of Staying Inside More 113
Making Bread for the First Time 114
Cookies for a Family Christmas Party 115

Haiku and Tanka Love Poems

116

Other Haiku and Senryu

117

Weather Changes

An Unforeseen Storm 121
Rainy Days 122
Storms Abound 123
The Weather People's Forecasts 124
The Temperature's Changing 124
The Hot Weather Blues 125
A Snowstorm in Early April 126
A Missed Thunderstorm 127

Better Days

Cinquains   128
Delighting in the Day   129
A Trip to the Beach   129

A Restaurant Customer

My husband and I checked out
of our room in Macon, Georgia
to journey seventy miles.

On this brisk morning, people
sought coffee warmth at the eatery
when a hooded visitor entered.

I glanced at him and noticed
his nose resembled my brother's;
his countenance looked weather-beaten.

With a hood covering his face
from the world, he appeared to want
no one to view his rough skin.

The stranger's skin needed moisture,
and he required compassion right then.
My husband handed him a lotion.

His address we didn't know,
or if he had employment.
Did anyone care for him?

The older man's spirit lifted,
saying, *Thank you* to my husband
for kindness and consideration.

We left that day, and I said,
I hope others show him concern.
At least the man's skin got some care.

Patricia Cruzan

Illinois's Storms

Downpours descend from the welkin at dust.
Tornadoes threaten Mount Vernon, Illinois.
White clouds vanish from the blackened sky
with winds blowing ceaselessly, out of the North.

Winter coats come out in early spring
to cut the chilliness of winter's last blast.
People hurry from cars to hotel rooms
in hopes of eluding the coming rain.

The beating rain advances on them,
setting the tone of what's amiss that night.
As tourists, they opt to stay in their room,
doing early morning preparations.

The next day starts with showers in the morning,
and winter clothes don bedewed bodies.
Visitors wear wraps from the howling winds,
protecting the body from nature's chill.

Stomach pangs recede as persons eat biscuits,
hash browns, eggs, meat, and drink grape juice.
Various fruits round out the food buffet
while coffee or water wash the food down.

Cars and large trucks barrel down the main road,
moving all kinds of items here and there.
The sun bursts forth with its radiant light,
and the sky exhibits cottony clouds.

As tourists drive ahead to their stopping place,
they seek food, fun, and lodging for that night.
Tomorrow, visitors' plans help them arrive
at destinations for viewing and resting.

The Topography of the East

The hills ascend in north Georgia,
and they continue soaring above
higher and higher they extend,
from a thousand to four thousand feet.

As a designer studies the land,
one visualizes how builders
hew through the rock to build
routes around each city.

Throughout the Virginia states,
pines and oaks are prominent,
and builders make the surfaces
of main roads for tourists' travels.

While going to Pennsylvania
and New York, the mountains get loftier
and steeper with scattered modest farms,
throughout the entire region.

Traveling to New York

Slight elevations abound
with emerald trees around.
People see tree after tree,
and they're thankful to be free
to admire verdant regions.
While roaming, watch for lions.
Fir trees surround every peak,
while inclines can make one bleak.

Tanka Poems

The River Thames

Tourists travel miles,
nearly two hundred, on banks
of the Thames, glimpsing
the river's dark and cloudy
at depths over twenty yards.

—

The Visitors of the Thames

Tourists stretch their legs
along a picturesque walk
to boat, fish, and dine.
A motor cruiser or barge
transports the adventurous.

Westminster Abbey

Westminster, a historical church,
is near Big Ben and parliament.
Remnants remind us of William
the Conqueror's coronation.

It's a beautiful site
of bygone people
who lived centuries ago
and made contributions.

Carnations number in the thirties,
making this church a cathedral
for royals to have a claim
for attending or receiving a crown.

A unique chair with graffiti
from children of yore's naughty scrawls
gets used for a royal's crowning,
as it did for St. Edward I.

Entombed and honored are Dickens,
Browning, and Shakespeare:
accomplished men of writings,
but others rest there too.

A Dome's Glory

A cathedral built long ago
  has levels one wants to scale.
The Whispering Gallery's acoustics
  makes people marvel at the construction,
along with the Stone Gallery's structure.
  The dome's cross and ball reach skyward.

The crypts and memorials honor men:
  heroes such as Wren and Nelson.
Though we don't know their motives,
  we know their talents and gifts
    as citizens of England.
  One chapel honors the Empire.

Patricia Cruzan

The Eiffel Tower

A marker standing high, we don't want to miss,
rises extra high in Paris, France for miles.
The immense black metal fabrication
causes you to admire varied buildings' styles.

It's riveting to view from different floors
with tiers showing more structures than other decks
as we look through a magnifier
people gaze long distances if we strain necks.

The shops around sell various goods,
and postcards are treasured from souvenir buys
from offered items in unique shops.
And when we leave there, we ask many whys.

Music and the Sidney Opera House

An invitation to an arts conference
allowed me to plan my Australian visit.
I knew travel might be a significant expense,
so my husband helped me to do research.

My partner booked me on a long flight
and helped to make my hotel booking.
I chose not to keep my case too light
as I had to take evening dresses and coats.

The nourishment in Sidney was unusual,
and I ate small portions before the concert night
until my stomach found it unsuitable
for having ethnic cuisine in my digestive parts.

I sang with the music in front of me
fondly, remembering most notes and words
as people listened and clapped hands with glee.
I'll always recall the other concert artists.

The Sidney Opera House was quite appealing
with its sails and reflection on the water.
The acoustics inside was very revealing
as singers' voices sang distinctly all over.

Mexico Recollections

Walking through the streets,
vendors seek your attention
as you journey west to east
for those attractive gifts.

Copper drinking cups
you want on your table
for drinks as you sup
in your eating area.

Some bargaining goes on
as you move about,
but stay clear at dawn
because vendors aren't ready.

A tan cloak looks fine
in reversible fabrics
and hems come with twine
to stay stitched for years.

The customer acquires it
while admiring the cape
and goes off to sit
before crossing the border.

The Virginia Landscape

White clouds in powder-blue skies
form above the horizon
over thick jade forests.

Billowy masses appear
over purple mountains,
towering above tall trees.

Diverse lands dot the terrain;
three crosses rise on a mound.
Rolling hills ascend upwards.

Tourists view shady mountains,
and gray-chiseled stones loom
against the ice-blue heavens.

No artists can attract
with pallets. Nature lures
with this panorama.

Patricia Cruzan

Travel Suggestions

When traveling, varied people journey for miles.
Tourists view truckers' loads while visitors give smiles.
Travelers use a kindness code and stay back awhile.

Carrying a thermos saves the cost of a drink.
Stop, so your kidneys don't burst, and your eyes blink.
Mixed nuts give protein, helping you think.

Hunger pangs make journeyers ready to eat.
You can get out of the car and use your feet
to walk from a peak and hear a song's beat.

The Drive to Emory Clinic

Five days a week, travelers go,
their journey on superhighways.
They follow the road just so,
keeping their distance from traffic.

People stay in their lane
to make a trip in one piece;
they go before there's pain
to get their treatments over.

The traffic moves along,
but no one travels too fast
as cars drive all day long
until brake lights radiate.

Stalled traffic takes time
while vehicles flood the road.
For the last treatment, a chime
gives evidence of the end.

Traveling in Town

As persons near the town,
the traffic gets much worse,
but it's not excessive
to shop for grocery needs.

Most customers are mask clad
and keep the six feet of distance
as they proceed aisle to aisle,
hoping the virus won't spread.

Assorted vehicles form
at traffic lights and stop signs,
but much congestion at junctions
usually doesn't exist.

At fast-food eating spots,
people pick up nourishment
for their abode that night,
rather than risk dining in.

Many think less chance exists
for coronavirus germs
to spread to other patrons
with few diners staying there.

Casual dining places
have more booths left empty
to provide for a six-foot distance
unless dining in high-back booths.

A Mountain Trip

A stream attracts with its flowing motion,
even though it contrasts with the salty ocean.
The allure of shady trees and rocks galore
makes us feel the beauty discovered before.

The hearth warms for those chilly nights coming,
making us happy as we keep on humming.
The logs give coziness to sustain our heat,
keeping the same temperature on our feet.

The wood looks new but isn't too dark;
with mini devices, we feel like a lark.
Since tourists have individual apartments,
there's plenty of room for undergarments.

There are two pools to go in on a whim
for those who take pleasure in taking a swim.
A child delights with the cooling refreshment
and moving, so he's not ever quiescent.

Hope for the Future

A rare movie ad arrived on my screen.
I longed to see the movie for weeks but was scared
because the Coronavirus took many lives.
The family wanted to observe a birthday
as masks came on, and people didn't sit close.
With concessions and coats, we sat far apart.

The feature shows sickness in a lady's body,
and she accepted cancer would take her life.
Friends furnished encouragement while the couple lived.
The lady didn't expect a stage four reading,
but her faith in God and mate dispelled fears.
The pair lived each day with God's promises.

Death took her life, but her husband relied on
words, trust, and faith he received from friends.
Gradually, care and time healed his heart.
The show reminded me of God's love for us.
The movie showed heaven and presented hope
of seeing loved ones and God's amazing love.

God Offers Hope

God furnished men with laws,
ten rules by Moses's hand
which man failed to obey,
living throughout the land.

Souls faced impulses,
refusing to let God mold
lives around the clock
so that Christians would be bold.

God punished and forgave
each time persons would sin,
but people always failed
until in Christ, they'd win.

Calvary's Redemption

A man tried to do what he could,
creating dissatisfaction.
God took away men's sins
by sending His son for compassion.

Christ was a sacrifice
for people throughout all time.
He died on a cross, even though
Christ committed no crime.

We earned salvation with His actions,
and by our acceptance, we'll live again
with Him in heaven among angels
and not just a has-been.

Death Long Ago on a Cross

The crossbeam Christ carried weighed a great deal
as He stumbled trying to hold it, another man
took it as Christ had no time to heal
from previous floggings of prison officers.

The nails pierced Jesus' side, hands, and feet
as He hung on that cross, suffering in anguish,
and Jesus had no meal since the Lord supper's feast
so that His body had no fluids to sustain Him.

Being crucified meant dying slowly
from dehydration and blood loss.
People withdrew so that He was lonely.
The Savior suffered while saying, *It's finished.*

Patricia Cruzan

What Life Might Be Like

When starting in life, people are a bit selfish
with time and money while furnishing houses.
People discipline themselves when beginning
because persons consider home and kin items.

Plans look daunting as one instructs children,
cleans house, cooks, shops, and makes a unique home.
People get wrapped up in doing many jobs
and having little time for natural living.

Persons send friendly cards for others' benefits;
and show the sender's love in others' lives.
Facebook posts let companions see your thoughts
of them in the greater scheme of life.

Life's not about only doing for ourselves
but helping others in their pursuit of living
because people need uplifting while facing problems
that are hard to bear without people's influence.

A Package Mailed

People mailed package kinds cheaply for years.
Now, you must have the correct box, paper, and label,
or you redo it for sending to its stopping place.

Dry ice mailing isn't available by most firms,
so persons mail-in cooler weather for unspoiled sweets.
Sending a priority package costs fifteen dollars.

The price for a larger parcel is expensive.
Even though one pays for priority mail,
the dispatch time is not known with countless boxes.

People don't understand all factors involved
in getting a container to someone.
The post office handles the final delivery.

A package arriving is fine to hear
when sending it out for comfort and cheer.
Persons like for relatives to know they care.

Neighbors Behind Hidden Doors

One neighbor used to visit regularly.
Her time with me was magnificent,
but then she pursued a degree,
and I took care of my sister
after a horrendous wreck.
Tasks kept us from socializing.

When a bad storm hit our property,
one person next door and his father
cleared broken limbs from trees
and hauled away fallen branches
which helped us out as neighbors.
The act displayed their concern.

Today, I speak to neighbors
while leaving on expeditions,
but seldom find the time to enter
into lengthy conversations.
At times when stopping for mail,
we halt for friendly remarks.

Young neighbors, on the other side,
have children outside when it's warm,
and if kids need help when we're there;
we try to help them with their plight.
Sharing children's magazines
was fun for the day we stopped.

The lady and husband seem shy,
and are much younger than us
as they work hard for their family,
there's seldom time for visits.
We often wave as we pass
while going uptown.

During the virus, I wish
for good health to neighborly families,
and that others will meet people's needs
as they go about living and working.
I want urgent needs for all persons
living in the world requiring help.

My Cousin

Her hair's silver and silky
       on sallow skin and small bones.

My cousin's sixty-eight pounds
       on her five-foot-eight frame.

Strong prescriptions manage
       the pain she feels for a while.

She drives her son from the market
       so that he doesn't trek home.

Mental pain grips her husband
       as he talks of life without her.

One spark of light she delights in
       before death comes from memories.

Mrs. Patel Finds Comfort

She walks with grace into the room;
her tiny feet clad in silky socks,
along with jet-black velvet shoes.
Her skirt sits below a tunic top.
She drapes a shawl from a shoulder.
Her diamond nose ring gleams to others.

While sitting, she dabs at her tears
with soft tissue, without a sound,
she sits until her spirit soothes.
Her eyes lift when a kind person
talks softly to get her attention.
With love, she speaks to the person.

Our drive from home is forty-five minutes;
we come from north Atlanta to Emory.
My mate endures pain from surgery,
and few days remain of his treatment.
Then her husband comes out, and she leaves.
She waves goodbye to a friend.

Days come and go before they meet;
her friend stays in the waiting room.
Mrs. Patel receives a book.
Her friend leaves as Mrs. Patel
waits. The friend doesn't see her for days
as the two don't meet in the waiting room.

Patricia Cruzan

Mrs. Patel's soul mate comes for treatment,
but her friend hears steps as she leaves.
Did you give me a book? Mrs. Patel asks.
Yes, her friend replies when she starts to leave.
The poems are lovely, she says to her friend.
Could you meet my relatives in the next room?

Mrs. Patel and her friend meet again.
The companion follows, hoping to give
Mrs. Patel support one last time,
as the two go with smiles and hugs,
from a chance encounter with a visitor.
And friends hope they've made a difference.

A Supper with My Brother

My gray-haired brother strums a guitar,
    sitting on wooden apartment steps,
    rehearsing music of the sixties.

Chords resound from lanky fingers;
    he wears a short-sleeved T-shirt, old blue jeans,
    with black leather slippers, slipped on his feet.

A missing-tooth grin and cerulean eyes
    greet me as feral cats purr softly before
    he changes to a name jean to dine with kin.

As he departs, his silver hair bounces
    while cats leap up to enter his abode,
    and he puts on his unique jeans and black loafers.

My husband purchases my brother a burger,
    soda, nuggets, and fries while we have
    burgers, cokes, and split a cookie.

A disheartened expression appears on his face
    when I leave for a high school meet-and-greet
    of friends absent for fifty-five years.

Patricia Cruzan

Kind Acts for a Special Loved One

Countless ways show your hubby your care,
but don't buy new clothes for him to wear.

A husband and wife share their bed each night;
they pull covers back and forth like they're out of sight.

To be romantic, they may write sweet notes,
and one avoids sickness by not going on boats.

A mate may do what one doesn't like to do
so that a spouse can rest and be good as new.

By taking a wife on a date to a film,
the mate can avoid a visit to the gym.

A present can be a day free from work,
where the spouse isn't, standing as a clerk.

A Homemade Quilt

An antique quilt sat in the closet
of varied colors: white, blue, burgundy,
tan, along with brown and gingham checks.
Small-scale, blue-striped triangles faced
three-sided angles in the reverse direction.
Grandmother's clients left her plenty of scraps.

Compact, red pieces made the quilt lively;
they offered the cover pigments and design.
Gray and tan triangles gave some contrast,
with ornate parts of burgundy and brown;
they formed a solid outer border.
On the opposite side, umber lined it.

Gramma stitched continuously for hours at a time
on crafts or sewing on a treadmill machine.
Whether she stitched for strangers, friends, or family,
she earned money for bills, rent, and pleasure.
Sewing furnished her much satisfaction
as she sewed for friends and newcomers.

Patricia Cruzan

Grandma's Cooking and the Cookie Jar

Grandma's chilled fruitcake excited me
with its nuts, candied fruit, and marshmallows.
I watched it enter the refrigerator
while my mouth drooled for its flavorful taste.

Mother cooked great recipes but never
used the same elements at any time of year.
I longingly gazed at Grandma's cake.
A previous quarrel between Grandma and Mother
caused me to slip the cake when Mom didn't see me.

I remember other things about Granny's kitchen,
such as the owl cookie jar, she always had there
with freshly baked goods for all to relish.
Its black eyes with brown circles and dark nose
glared at a distance in the room when I walked there.
Its decorative flowers on the middle and top
often had goodies waiting inside.

I treasured what awaited me when she opened it,
and I never felt disappointed with its contents.
Years went by, and she gave the jar to me,
and I have fond memories of surprises inside.
I seldom use the heirloom for fear of breaking it,
but it's nestled in my kitchen for guests to notice.

My Family as an Adult

God heard my prayer for companionship;
He answered with love, given from above.
My heart broke from a previous romance.
The fellow needed, not even a glance.

After sixteen marriage months, my son appeared;
he suffered from colic but was superb.
He spat out food, but he made our life fun;
right before pictures, he'd take off and run.

When he was a teen, he worked at a restaurant:
cooking, serving, cashiering, and cleaning.
Friends affected his behavior and dress.
He's learned now not to keep rooms in a mess.

After age thirty-eight, he bought a house;
makeovers changed it all over.
He bought a truck but may need a van
for hauling things off as a mature man.

Patricia Cruzan

Eating with Family

Step into a luscious café.
Lines form, waiting to get in
for entrees, veggies, and desserts.
Customers enter with kin.

They're waiting for a choice plate
that is fresh and fills them up.
Healthy food helps all bodies,
and our drinks will fill each cup.

Persons slowly digest food,
using their social skills.
Being with other people
lifts one's spirit and gives frills.

The Gift of Friends

What will the new year bring?
Will friends cause one to sing?

Friends make life sublime;
soul mates add zest divine.

Some people waste one's time
while others stay at their prime.

Persons urge jobs with low pay,
but workers seek trades to stay.

Cards offer cash for living
and other gifts one's giving.

Relief helps friends feel new,
so be nearby for them, too.

Patricia Cruzan

The Reunion

The meet-and-greet meeting enticed
    faces from decades ago.
        Concise exchanges commenced.

 Background music played constantly,
    reminding choral performers
        of times before leaving high school.

Fine students and football film
    showed prior years activities
        before shrimp and steak arrived.

Couples relished potatoes,
    green beans, triangular brownies,
        sprinkled tiny cakes, and cookies.

Discussions stopped with others,
    when a coach of ninety rose;
        he stood for recognition.

High school friends drifted away,
    as unobtrusive remarks
        sounded, and the night faded.

Valiant People

Bravery comes in all proportions and shapes,
and one might be fearless in fighting disease,
attacking for freedom, or combating evil.
A war might begin here or overseas.

Soldiers carry arms, keeping freedom alive,
for liberties we need, where fighters may be.
We cherish these freedoms won by troopers,
aiding our country, so citizens are free.

Doctors fight illness for humans and faunas,
keeping us healthy to live longer lives
so that people can stay at their very best
to achieve ambitions and daily drives.

Persons want to leave appealing legacies.
Pastors lead lives of selfless devotion,
preaching, and teaching from God's Holy Word
with sermons that show much time and emotion.

Podiums or lecterns carry their notes
as preachers make people aware of sin.
Congregants listen as ministers preach
how good will triumph as God will win.

The Internet's Pros and Cons

Ideas arrive in our heads while writing,
and by using a search engine, we get details
about our history, science, or most any topic.
Individuals have access instantly
in a fingertip world of knowledge.
Instead of getting a library book,
facts come quickly; we need them for writing.

When emails come in, they're various kinds
and plenty of clutter to wade through for value.
Others have access to private addresses
and deluge us with items that we don't need.
Phone calls come in from here and far,
asking for aid to charities and politics.
Callers frequently use spoofed numbers.

If humans aren't careful, they'll give away
details to strangers lurking for knowledge
to make their living at the expense of all
they meet through emails and phone calls.
Numbers not recognized might or might not
need to be answered at that exact moment.
People can leave messages for necessary calls.

The Coronavirus

Suddenly, persons get sick with symptoms;
a respirator helps if problems come.
Everywhere earthlings move forward,
a mask covers the mouth and nose
with a six-foot distance between persons.

Stores take precautions by keeping folks
apart by six feet on floors with tape.
Small-scale screens shield check-out clerks
from customers in hopes of providing safety,
and buyers feel secure with an extra divider.

Eating places have tables spaced further,
creating the suggested interval for dining.
High-booth backs with people facing away
provide for the well-being of patrons.
Servers run rapidly from table to table.

The Sun's Out

The sun shines in Georgia,
so it must be warm,
is a view people have
but leads to an alarm.

When stepping out,
people fail to change clothes.
They think what they select
will last before they doze.

Outside attire
may consist of a sweat
with shorts and tennis shoes
without any fret.

Others may put on,
heavy shirts and pants
because of degrees,
they take a chance.

The Past Election

People go through stress to get out and vote,
but have they prepared for their cast ballot?
Maybe the party before the one now
is farther to the right or left in dealings.

Beings form views from ads and articles;
they don't always present things as they are.
An incident reporter might lack all facts
to present real stories just as they are.

Persons get tired of the status quo
and want a chance to see if things improve,
not always looking at all the facts,
but think a change might help the government.

Time will tell with the leader's choices made
who the better leader is in handling affairs
for the people's welfare under their command,
or their influence as a human does their job.

Patricia Cruzan

Not Considering Things Fast Enough

Persons do errands quickly
so that they can complete other tasks.
While moving about, humans try
to achieve several things before sitting.

It's difficult at times to recall
all reasons regarding why one's up,
so people do what they remember
and then settle before getting up.

People hasten to finish chores
not recalled before taking a chair.
Once seated, an individual
may rise to do tasks forgotten.

By the time one returns for sitting,
people don't have as much energy
to complete chores as they did prior.
Work continues, but not as fast.

Obstacles to Being Blind or Partially Deaf

People born blind can't see the director,
leading the orchestra and depending on others
to drive them to the locale as a musician.
Using a set of ears for changes isn't easy
since the director frequently alters tempos.

Walking is challenging, with potholes
while traveling on streets, lower places, or paths.
Without functioning eyes, braille books are essential.
If a large dog comes up, a blind person strives
to prevent hard knocks and getting bitten.

If one can't hear clearly, phone calls are hard
because missing words will prevent one from getting
instructions your doctor or others might give.
Friends don't know when hearing aids are out,
but a partially deaf person tires with phone use.

Background noise prevents hearing plainly,
so all exchanges could have missing letters
and phrases needed for communication
appropriately to questions and statements made.
Preciseness is required for the hearing impaired.

Living with Criticism

Before sleeping, words heard before
kept me awake and gnawed at me.
The reading left an imprint in my mind;
I grasped the story's words like a bee.

As the part unfolded, grogginess took over,
and remarks became blurred on the novel's page.
I finished the chapter as I persisted
and deduced the character's new life stage.

A remark inched into my mind before sleeping,
but the need for rest took over my head,
and I drifted to sleep from the day's fatigue,
not thinking of the day from which I'd fled.

A Nature Walk

I wandered
by blooms reflecting
in a pond
standing still.
A small duck broke the silence,
gracefully swimming.

-

A Farm Visit

An inky-necked horse stops still
with his black tail and dark mane,
standing motionless on the lea.

A myriad of flowers: Blue,
yellow, and pink, in rows
attract photographers' eyes.

Shutterbugs shoot photos
of bright blooms and chickens,
standing straight and clucking.

A brown-spotted dog submits
to its owner, waiting for its friend,
a gray mongrel appears.

Photographers crouch down,
trying for picture-perfect shots
while chickens continue to crow.

Deer Habits

A baby doe peers in a glass door
and sees no way to get inside,
so he gazes a minute and then rests.
His ears go up for scary sounds.

I wonder what the deer thinks of his closeness
to humans as he gets in a crescent shape.
On other days, some deer visit foliage,
far away from distant persons in woods.

Do more gaps make them feel more comfortable?
Or do they think they can move safely fast?
Nibbles from afar seem to work for them,
but I'd like them up-close to see them.

If beings get too close, deer gallop
into forest regions of underbrush
or so far into woods, and persons don't see them.
After things are tenebrous outside, deer roam.

The Wild Turkeys

A flock of turkeys comes to visit in the fall;
they look pretty erect, and we're glad they call.
Their bodies have feathers in shades of brown,
and they don't even wear a delightful crown.

Turkeys move slowly and wobble back and forth;
they peck the ground regularly, going North.
Seeds we don't see, the game birds seem to find,
and they don't mind people if they're kind.

A Rabbit Seeks Flora

A brown rabbit hops in grasses
while munching on verdant lawns,
filling its empty stomach.

A car engine sends it scurrying
to plentiful pine forests,
away from a person's motor.

It hides in the underbrush
with its beautiful, nut-brown eyes
to watch if it has to leap.

The mammal looks for flora
while listening to the engine,
and it waits to return to the turf.

Birds and Mates

Birds call out for mates
but don't have first dates.
People don't know what tweets say
or what they try to convey.

Plumed friends build sundry nests;
on your porch, they are pests.
Chirps persist with mates found
as they fly all around.

-

Feathered Friends Seek Lunch

Birds with long necks stroll;
while gawking, they get sticks.
Before diving in the water,
they don't exhibit kicks.

When they start to fish,
birds' bills grasp lunch.
Feathered friends have patience
while seeking out a bunch.

The Porch's Bird Nest

I see moss on a porch light,
nothing else looks altered,
so I speak of plants to my husband.
A study reveals the birds' nest.

The roost shows three blue eggs;
the mother settles on them.
Mini mouths open for food
as the mom brings fare to mouths.

The following spring, birds come back,
hoping to build a nest.
To prevent a porch mess,
my spouse derails their plans.

The Swooping Owl

There's always a different vista to see
when gazing outside and looking at a cloud.
Suddenly, an owl swoops from a tree,
and it quickly goes forward as if proud
to fly farther South to a contrasting lea.

The size of the owl caught me by surprise
while he comes near with its enormous body,
perfecting bending its wings through the skies,
soaring toward the heavens as if it's cocky
until it lingers for a specific prize.

Bernie, the Dog

Old Bernie of Fayetteville
wandered the city's streets.
It stole food from a grill,
cooking all sorts of meats.

While running, it heard a song,
and the dog listened to a pop.
It left when hearing a gong
and went with a jump and hop.

Bernie yearned for a bone
while seeking to be content.
He sought to get it alone
without any lament.

Since Bernie lost bones before,
the dog hurried for a chance,
to grab a steak bone and explore
moves to make for an advance.

Mister Fry stepped up front,
getting meat from the fridge.
Bernie thought out his stunt
before going to the bridge.

The bone provided delight
while gathering food that night.
Bernie hoped for no fight
and saw no dogs in sight.

A Cornered Hedgehog

The barking points out an inquiry's needed,
so the owner goes out to the canine's pen.
The hedgehog trembles at the front.
The retriever's bark shows how proud it is
while the hedgehog doesn't move at all.

A shovel removes the hedgehog;
it vanishes, and the golden calms.
The quietude returns without
the visitor. The dog settles and rests
in its pen for the night. The owner goes back
to bed, seeking peaceful sleep in the darkness.

Patricia Cruzan

An Unusual Rescue

The morning started as normal
with tasks performed as usual
when the golden started barking
as I worked on a renewal.

The yelp got muffled, I noticed,
so I rushed to see the reason.
I figured an animal must be,
getting in its pen or region.

I saw no cause for woofing
until I peered at the end.
In its mouth sat a small snake,
and I knew I had hands to lend.

I seized a shovel in the garage
and lifted it to the dog's snout;
in my soul, I felt such happiness,
but I kept from emitting a shout.

The snake welcomed the release
into a wooded area
where it could hunt for food
and not face such hysteria.

The Cat's Hideouts

A neighbor cried out for her cat,
but it stayed invisible to her.
Owners didn't see the tom leave
and glanced outside to look for it.

A senior man discovered it
in the dog's old garage home.
The young neighbor ceased calling
the cat, and the gloaming came.

The gentleman frightened the cat,
so it left running down the street.
The feline strayed far and yonder,
seeking food and ties to strangers.

For several days, it rested
on our front porch in the sun,
and the cat went there 'for days
until the man frightened it.

The Brightness of Orange

The sun over the water
shows as yellow and orange.
As it emerges brighter,
its radiance shines skyward.

Orange pumpkins are silent,
but the hue catches the eyes
as the brightness glows around,
we can't help noticing them.

Pumpkins are squishy inside
while the outside shells look firm.
The surface and center yield
a contrast for our touch sense.

The taste isn't like other fruits.
There's nothing to compare it to,
for appearing on fall's crisp days,
so kids enjoy the season, too.

-

The Effect of Colors

The ice-blue sky appears calm
as puffy clouds float along,
then light dispersion sends
a vivid rainbow.

Sky-blue items imply peace,
not like rising yeast,
while orange suggests action
for leaping ahead with tasks.

How Colors Affect People

A calming effect comes upon us
as the blue of the sky surrounds souls.
White-filled clouds shift direction
as refraction makes rainbows:
A color arch streams to the earth.

Sky-blue commodities soothe
while red hints of maneuvers nearby.
Green refreshes the psyche
as plants sprout anew each spring.
Goldenrods bring brightness.

Silver-gray skies predict rain;
wet weather produces food.
Nut-brown colors hint of autumn
with pitch-black nights appearing soon
and sleep for people's stamina.

Gardening

Sea green hues make things look new
while staring at plants laden with dew.

Edible plants are often pea green;
on a pod, they appear like a bean.

Often humans wear a beat-up jean
to work at gardening, making plants green.

Green thumb gardeners work in spring,
hoping for what their labor will bring.

-

White Objects

Christmas baubles of snowy angels
help us remember protective messengers;
their milky robes and hair stand for virtue.

Beached sand against the azure ocean
gives a softness to the deep blue waters.
With the sun's rays, the sand looks like diamonds.

White polyester curtains provide
a brightness, letting in subdued light
while keeping things obscure within the room.

The Color Blue

When we see blue articles,
they catch our field of vision.
Does blue impart a restfulness?
While viewing the ice-blue sky,
the hue creates serenity.

Blue doesn't cry out
like red for attention,
yellow, pink, and orange.
It's attractive on clothes,
walls, or outside siding.

Ocean water seems blue
and calls to us to relax
by swimming or standing
in nature's crashing waves.
Tension leaves the body
after enjoying nature.

The Color Gray

Dimness often pervades winter days
as skies never lighten in midday.
Gloomy rain clouds often form on cold days,
darkening rooms and causing pensiveness.
Mortals depend on their faith in God
and others to bring them through shadowy times.

Connections and prayers can provide a closeness
to the Creator and friends of faith;
therefore, companions may meet at Zoom meetings,
making contact with others and get knowledge.
Encouragement may come with kindred traits,
or listening to others who need our help.

—

Red Gets Your Attention

A red truck stands out while traveling in traffic
as it's easy to see while looking at wheels
of assorted colors, and red grabs eyes.

Red stands out as fire trucks race ahead
to where there's a need to put out flames.
Police use red as a warning of danger.

Ambulance sirens race with red lights
to show the urgency for medical help
for victims in vehicle or work accidents.

The blinking red light denotes a stop,
so notice comes before an intersection
to make sure all watch for traffic hazards.

Seeing the Color Brown

Humans perceive the color brown a lot
if they glimpse at things in the out-of-doors world
as leaves plummet from trees in the autumn
and sometimes travel in a twirl.

People observe the bark and tree branches,
appearing dark brown to their eyes.
Trees are an excellent contrast for viewing
with towering trunks to the skies.

Horse saddles catch our artistic attention
with designs created by artists on them.
As riders ascend to start a journey,
others like to stop and ogle the gem.

Frequently, nut-brown boots stand out
when ranchers mount horses for going riding.
They soon hope to return to the home ranch
with the horse consistently moving and minding.

In homes, we see various kinds of furniture
shades of varied browns with window views,
and when we go to church, parishioners might see
a lectern, guitars, and many pews.

Black Items

Persons don't see black easily;
some remain dim, not seeable.
Dark trees and grasses go unseen
as they don't show in the darkness.

Stars give little light in the distance.
With lights, people see black pants,
blouses, shirts, and dresses;
and other colors give a disparity.

Formalwear is often black
so keep a suit on your rack.
We wear it not to stand out,
but in respect for others.

Yellow Brightens the Day

The trumpet-shaped blooms
brighten up our rooms
as daffodils
freshen each space.

The rays of the sun
make you want to run
outside for a picnic
in the brilliant day.

Walls of yellow
are like a meadow
with wildflowers
embellishing the earth.

Yellow garb is seeable,
making it feasible
for crossing guards to use
to help kids cross streets.

Fall Arrives

The days of summer subside
with ninety degrees of heat;
temperatures of seventy
arrive in mid-October,
followed by forty degrees.
Hot and humid days vanish,
and intense beams of the sun.

Gray skies replace dazzling days,
where it looks as if it might drizzle.
Artificial lights give brightness
which helps with all kinds of writing
on paper or computer.
Writers want their work understood
for education and leisure.

Pumpkins and Costumes for Halloween

Youngsters clad in fairy tale garb,
witch, transformer, and ghost attire,
saunter up toward neighbors' doors.
Orange rind pumpkins light a path
to effulgent stoops for guests to see,
strolling in costume to front doors.

Masks provide a disguise
so that trick-or-treaters have fun;
joyful children open sacks,
hoping for candy or treats.
As people lean in to give gifts,
smiling children's faces melt hearts.

-

An Orange-Yellow Fruit

At Halloween, people carve,
scooping pulp to make faces:
Various kinds for the pumpkin.
Orange-yellow flavoring goes in
spices, rolls, and coffee creams.
The pumpkins' orange-jagged grins
brighten brown leaves and gray skies
while mingling with the surroundings.

Thanksgiving Memories

Before dawn, Mom always cooked a turkey,
gravy, pecan, and fruit pies. She made
salads, vegetables, ambrosia,
and bread for a sumptuous meal for parents,
brothers, sisters, and other visitors.

For the family meal, I prepared a turkey,
dressing, salad, and vegetables.
Dishes tasted tangy with assorted spices
and onions added flavor to vegetables
and meats for the Thanksgiving feast.

Gone are days when I cooked all dishes
for the Thanksgiving holiday.
Now, menu items greet diners seeking
the first-class fare without doing the complete
work of cooking for hours on end.

Blessings for Thanksgiving

People forget to give thanks
but have blessings for today.
Food, friendship, and enjoyment
come from humans we hold dear.
We're grateful for health each day
for friends who live in nursing homes,
hospitals, or have died.

Sizeable homes provide room
for out of season clothing,
to go up front
while others are accessible.
Doors in separate closets
keep spring and summer clothes
stored away until needed.

Winter Arrives

Layers and layers of clothes come on
to blot out the chill in the air outside
while humans hustle to avoid the cold,
until the car heater warms the air.

Cars, SUVs, and trucks line the drive
before the patient reaches the lift.
With a minute to spare, the lady signs in;
then her husband holds the coat she's shed.

The receptionist hands the woman a form
partly filled out for the lady to check.
Signatures go on the other documents;
then reading follows until the nurse comes.

The nurse and doctor question the patient
until it's time for her to check out.
Following appointments go on her calendar
as she merrily does the next errand.

An Icy Blast

The weather's in the forties,
and temperatures drop so low
into the teens and twenties.

The wind whips around flags
as vermilion stripes stand out
with the breeze waving Old Glory.

The chain on the pole resounds
while the wind pushes the banner,
and gales get more robust.

An extra thickness of clothing
blots out bitter temperatures
as the sturdy physique heats up.

A thick hood cuts out gusts,
and gloves protect fingers,
for fighting winter's iciness.

Added clothes are bulky,
but garments keep one cozy
from chills of blustery winds.

Patricia Cruzan

Christmas Is Upon Us

The domestic work begins
by scrubbing walls and floors.
And thoughts turn to the inn
where Jesus came from barn doors.

We clean papers from rooms
to open gifts
and think of the wise men,
laying treasures from no lists.

Regular chores await us
for wives and husbands, too.
We know of Christ's endurance
and of what He went through.

The baking still needs doing
for the Christmas party.
Our minds recall Christ's love;
his messages, He declared smartly.

The tree stands for trimming
for the pleasure of all to see,
denoting the life eternal
the Lord gives us to be free.

Decorating the Christmas Tree

Tree limbs stand tall with white lights
and red encircled roping.
Decorations are varied
while the tree is like the King.

The lights represent Jesus
amid the world's darkness.
The ornaments add interest,
but our focus is on lights.

As we attach tree trimmings,
we can't let worldly things
deflect from Jesus' birth
as a significant event.

Patricia Cruzan

Christmas Wrappings

The tissue papers of red and gold
sit nearby, waiting to be chosen
while assorted bags one can't hold
lie near the wrapper, as if frozen.

Four golden harps from a theme park
add glitter and brightness to unique gifts.
Time and patience give packages a spark
with nimble fingers and a twist of the wrists.

Medium felt bags make the perfect gift wrap
for a gift's shape; one doesn't care to cover.
Always remember that jolly, old chap
as friends open presents and seek to hover.

Youngsters will try for their best behavior
so that toys will turn up on Christmas Day.
People will want to honor the Savior
who taught persons how to have faith and pray.

-

Christmas Nights

The tree shows off lights
that glow throughout the nights,
and the star on top shines down
as it beams throughout the town.
By selecting certain kin's gifts,
friendliness comes through, and no rifts.
The hostess serves lots of food
to create a festive mood.
As a tree shows a white dove,
people share relatives' love.

Gifts for Writers

Gifts for writers differ:
Books, computers, and pens
supply hours of joy,
as literary tools,
and notable tomes on style
help them write future novels.

Gifts of plants may not work
unless they get ample care
to thrive in varied states;
writers move them for water
since authors lose track of time,
spending hours on plots.

Distinctive writers proceed,
such as fictional authors,
or dog lovers penning books
about how to care for canines
so that pets will grow and thrive.
Affection shows in their hug.

Ornaments or Jewels

When the world views adornments
on others' outward windows,
the trimmings exude a brightness.

A person who shines from within
can transform things around them
to actions rather than show.

Mortals should observe closely
a rare jewel may pass by
who silently waits to shine.

A New Year

Determining how the new year goes
seems optimistic with a vaccine
for healthcare workers and the public.
With masks, social distancing, and shots,
people aren't fearful of grocery shopping
and combing department store aisles for objects.

Going places provides scenery changes
so that humans feel refreshed in new areas.
Seeing varied items will supply chances
to use senses to take in what's around,
for keeping the brain active as one takes in
diverse sights from what's seen and heard at home.

People see the food they don't think of eating
since shopping online allows no food contact.
Eating new food groups can make us healthy
to get vitamins for a fit body.
Our taste buds respond to different food,
and our life outlook improves with altered meals.

Patricia Cruzan

Groundhog Day

The groundhog saw his shadow this year,
causing us to believe there were six winter weeks.
People endured the prediction and wore
heavy clothes for working and shopping for days.

Low temperatures made us pine for early spring
to be milder so that fewer clothes went on.
Persons wished for various store items.
High temperatures spoiled us for some days.

Valentines in February

People give valentines to their spouse
on February the fourteenth, and to friends whether
qualities they have are superb or faulty.

Our wishes go online to people we don't see,
and cards go out to family and companions
who like encouragement in the world of today.

The valentine expresses our love
and like the ruby rose usually is pleasing
to the eye to attract our attention and ego.

Cerise frills and lacey trims add beauty
to boxes with candy just waiting for our taste,
along with a lovely card for us to read.

A post online reminds others we consider
them to be vital to get greetings from us.
The note lets them know they're crucial in our lives.

Patricia Cruzan

Young Love

One couple marries after months of an engagement
while yet another girl commits with a ring.
It's pleasant to experience happiness with dreams.
The sparkle of a new ring brings a facial smile,
as people recall getting an engagement ring.

An older person knows the marriage highs and lows,
but the engaged one's joy always is bubbly.
The engagement reminds us of what it is like
to start a journey with a future mate.
Planning entails outlining tiny matters.

People accomplish plenty when they're young
and energy seems boundless as they do tasks.
Early planning for children is best before old age
because there's more zest in adulthood's first years;
tolerance appears to be greater without pain.

Wisdom comes with experiencing a great deal,
and people advise those who need their help
in managing their lives, starting with the marriage.
Spending less for a wedding means more for essentials
to make daily living happy for those involved.

March Beginnings

As March starts to draw nigh,
we search for signs of spring;
flowers sprout, and pollen
forms, winds blow regularly,
and ice-blue skies appear.

Gone are the gray, drab days
where thermometers hit thirty,
and people want milder days
of brightness and newness on Earth;
the world takes on a fresh look.

Since the sun rises earlier
with the light creeping at dawn,
humans arise with fervor
of completing errands swiftly
while the luminescence increases.

Efforts begin readily
as the light provides a clear view,
of details that stand before us
while doing projects, we take on;
longer days increase work.

Patricia Cruzan

A Breath of Spring

When enchanting songs greet me in spring,
and pollen coats my street, walk, and car.
I think of what my day will bring
while watching spring limbs shift near and far.

The sun casts its beams through windowpanes,
inviting me outside to feel its heat
to wander through meadows, fields, and lanes
or relax out of doors and take a seat.

Gentle breezes caress my skin
while sweeping grasses and leaves to the side.
Puffs of air spread seeds in a spin;
kernels drift away to glide and hide.

I turn to hear a bird call out.
The warbler keeps singing like a songstress,
and I want to sing with a shout.
The bird stands out because of its headdress.

Is Spring Finally Here?

It's sixty-eight degrees outside.
Is spring coming in fearlessly?
Or is it entering slowly
to wear three-quarter sleeve tops?

The sun radiates,
enhancing Earth with brightness
against ethereal skies
as shadows pass from foliage.

It stays light out longer.
Seeds sprout numerous colors
of pink, yellow, and purple
over the landscape.

No brisk winds blow outside
as one adjusts to the glow.
Powdery grains cover cars,
making them like two colors.

Spring Is Around the Corner

Yellow-centered white flowers
stand against green stems,
near bunched deciduous trees.

Six milky petals protect
inside tiers: one white
and golden inner parts.

-

Appealing Blooms

Cup-shaped, colorful flowers
encircle the mailbox:
lemon, scarlet, and pink.
Six satiny bold petals
greet guests with extended stems
ascending, like lilies, bloom
from March through May of each year.

Spring: A Time of Changes

The wind kicks up lightly,
increasing before the change.
Breezes occur nightly,
and the weather seems strange.

Lilies split open heads
through earth's inky ground
while emerging from beds
without a single sound.

When spring weather comes near,
people build a tire swing.
While having fun this year,
people will try to sing.

A Mother Celebrated

People cherish their mother
because there is no other
one who gives lots of drive
to make sure that we thrive.

Humans honor them for feeding
and help us with our reading,
so we learn lessons in school
and practice the golden rule.

Nine months, Mom carries us
and then, tends us when we fuss
to meet each single need
for us to grow like a weed.

Fathers' Qualities

Fathers are boulders,
giving strength; they
are thankful people
for whatever happens.

Fathers give aid,
assisting wives
in getting rest
by doing taxing tasks.

Dads go shopping
with mothers to help
and take their kids
to toy stores to look.

Fathers take leave,
building a bond
as they model a soul
that God supplies.

Dads solve problems,
providing answers;
they use discernment
and pearls of wisdom.

Fathers pray for
a family's plight,
providing guidance
inside and beyond.

Patricia Cruzan

Summers of the Young

Nights of summers slipped away—
nights of lightning bugs and beetles.
Outdoor lights attracted bugs,
dancing and landing all over
while dogs slept out, not hidden
in hot, dank kennels, too close.

After seventeen or eighteen summers,
young people graduated.
They strolled in sandy winds,
causing gritty hair like rope strings.
The breaking waves hit the shore,
drowning out vows to the engaged.

Despite college detachments,
young ones delighted in the joy
without thinking of tomorrow.
Then in seclusion, notions
changed to the busy schedule,
leaving no time for reflections.
Busyness replaced pensive studies.

Returns from a get-away called
for answers to another question:
What is life like now?
Questions droned on —inquiries
not wanted, creating vexation
until students were free, at last.

Activities for the Summer

Swimming lessons in summer
can make you a hummer.

The learning of a skill
can give you an exact thrill.

Not only does one cool off,
swimming averts one's scoff.

Picnicking gets you out
to view water from a spout.

Ambling at a slow pace
helps you see a pretty place.

While rafting, you're in the sun,
and you welcome rest when done.

Patricia Cruzan

The Fair at a Church

Booths of jewelry, blankets,
pecans, pens, mugs, and photos
line the gym for purchasers,
looking for unique wonders.
Green and violet pendants
along with earrings,
attract eyes to displays.

Vendors refine pitches,
pointing out product features.
Youth and elders buy gifts
for friends and neighbors.
Poetry and children's books
exist for the keen reader
and for those who like novels.

Life Perspectives

A Festival with Many Vendors

A gold and turquoise necklace
    on a ceramic cream bust
    attracts a blue-eyed lady
    and brown hair of middle age.

A woman buys a long necklace
    and gazes at brilliant portraits
    on flexible wires and clips,
    and compact salad bowls.

Vivid floral arrangements
    reside by earrings
    as shoppers shop for treasures
    of copper, gold, and silver.

Ceramics of blue and red
    entice lingering looks,
    to view attractive racks
    which hold large, wooden bowls.

Customers look at replicas
    of canines, deer, horned owls,
    and 3D snowmen,
    waiting for buyers to purchase.

Wind and brass musicians
    perform euphonic melodies
    with the young and old,
    making up an orchestra pit.

A Book Festival

The clowns, balloons, and writers
sit waiting with costumes and treats,
while famous and well-known authors,
perform their encouraging feats
of getting persons to browse.

Children dawdle in on stilts,
seeking an autograph.
Their way of searching for books
makes writers chatter and laugh
as lines go around for signings.

Fingers let go of balloons,
sending them up to the ceiling
where parents help kids retrieve,
no matter how they're feeling.
Children's grins become priceless.

Authors at the Decatur Book Festival

A large box arrives of books to a door.
With vibrant covers, an author hopes to score
scores of readers at the Decatur Book Fair
as numerous writers are there to share.

Browsing customers appear at last,
one hardly knows where a book's cast.
After one talks, showing their labor,
an author might talk to a neighbor.

Shoppers pick out a stylish gift,
and in a minute, eyes may shift.
Book buyers find novels they like best,
and an author doesn't squelch their zest.

Customer sales make authors happy
and time is precious, so buyers are snappy.
If you want to know how to publish a book,
start to develop a unique hook.

Authors write and study on a computer,
and a writer doesn't have to be a bus commuter.
One can type a concept to see what he finds,
and details will come from several minds.

Patricia Cruzan

Budgeting Time

Mortals have the same amount of time each day
to accomplish work and art throughout the hours,
but some make more progress than others working
at their livelihood and crafts they like.

Young people start work early in the day
while older persons finish their nightly rest.
People in their twenties sleep without effort,
and older people have splendid and awful nights.

Daily, people make time for chores and artistry
so that a balance causes one to get jobs done.
By spending a little time on tasks and crafts,
persons accomplish work and art without boredom.

Finding Time to Write

Some days one needs more hours
while other days are all right.
The time a person travails
may lead throughout the night.

The laundry needs attention
with heaped-up piles and mounds.
When washers start their cycle,
one may need several rounds.

A ding breaks the silence
as people start other work.
Clothes need drying later;
one gets up with a jerk.

An author takes things slowly
while building a written piece;
sentence-construction takes time,
and revision doesn't cease.

Paper placed close at hand
can help a writer out.
Thoughts may easily vanish
and an author may sit and pout.

When an idea appears,
jot it down before your life
consumes every minute,
or something causes strife.

Take some moments each day
to find joy in a craft,
because life's full of woes,
but don't leave on a raft.

Creating a Poetry Book

Writing a book seems a simple feat,
but a writer must follow countless steps.
A poet needs over a hundred poems
for a book-length manuscript and thirty
to fifty poems for a chapbook.

All writings fit under a topic an author
makes for grouping like subjects together.
An author may revise many times for correctness.
The publisher's staff checks for spacing and page numbers.
A cover picture or artist creates book appeal.

Page number and poem checks begin anew.
The publisher makes sure there are no mistakes
before a printer begins work on a book.
The publisher looks over the collection again
for printing imperfections and errors.

A book arrives after months of production,
and a reader enjoys reading poems at their pace.
No matter the intent, poems satisfy.
A poetry book makes readers regard like
and different views about life in general.

Spectators at a Fair

The morning begins with the usual
of setting up and displaying.
Shoppers look around to inspect
jewelry, stuffed animals, and books
for buying from contrasting vendors.

The distinct purchasers are
gift buyers and book lovers.
At times, people want to look,
or stop to get publishing facts,
or halt for a gripping item.

Authors don't mind helping some,
but avoid cornering a writer,
because authors want to sell.
People seeking advice take up room
for customers to check exhibits.

Writers are happy to aid authors
with a limited amount of time,
but buyers need room to inspect,
since sales assist in paying
the display spaces for writers.

Using Our Eyes

Bright light adds clarity to see,
helping us enjoy what life brings.
Writers use the sun at sea
to watch gulls use their wings.

Beams give a specific glow,
providing us with light.
Great authors' works are slow,
as they toil into the night.

Pieces are easy to read
from writings formed in bright light.
Writers indeed take the lead
to do things with all their might.

Authors without a clear view
have tools vanish for a spell.
Gadgets may recede in dew,
so guard them outside well.

Writers view things in the light
while staring at nature on Earth.
Objects may not appear bright,
but authors aim for words of worth.

Ice Cream Treats

Ordering food isn't always easy
as people line up at ninety degrees.
Clerks take requests for sizes and flavors.

Persons choose from different kinds of tastes
while temperatures ascend in south Georgia.
So many flavors make choosing difficult.

Air conditioners run while souls are there,
but they want comfort every part of the day.
After being inside, one welcomes the sun.

People leave the eating place to get in cars
for their ride back home to perform duties
and seek amusement for those around.

Patricia Cruzan

The Usefulness of House Rooms

Consider your room use when buying a house.
In today's society, people want lots of space.
They think of the family room for fun,
and how much of your time you spend in that room.

People reflect on kitchen time for the day
as they consider cooking, eating, and cleaning it.
Length of time in the room may surprise one
with extra trips, water, and cooking needs.

Restrooms get their use through the day
for disposing of wastes inside bodies there.
People avail themselves of showers or tubs
to keep the body free from dirt and germs.

Rooms for sleeping supply places for rest
and chests, as well as a closet for garments.
Other spots in the house are presentable for friends
or family coming inside for a chat.

Dining rooms furnish just enough space
for china cabinets and tables for guest eating
without being too large for extra space to clean,
so owners can enjoy other spacious rooms.

Bonus rooms supply an expanse for computers,
shelves, printers, writing cabinets,
paper, books, and display tables,
ready for work or entertainment.

The Chair

The brown leather chair invites,
presenting plump arms and padded back.
A mechanical lever lifts
sore legs and tired-out feet.
The chair's well-rounded arms
help one relax for a break.

There's a place for a water cup
that quenches people's thirst
while people watch a show,
or sit cleaning some drawers.
Correspondences with friends
occur in the chair daily.

Too much time in the chair
can cause unfinished chores
and not doing devotions.
Family needs nurturing,
and prayers ascend each day
to God for those we love.

Patricia Cruzan

Little Things Mean a Lot

Paint in some rooms made them look superior,
and new wall plates made spaces seem brighter.

Changing out thirty-year-old ones with new plates
improved the whole appearance of territories.

Fresh paint brightened walls and new plates
added contrasts to walls needing a change.

Instead of a drabness where people suspected dirt,
walls looked more attractive with current colors.

One day when looking, I saw present-day plates
shining in rooms with fresh coats of paint.

No one realizes how many wall plates
they need in a room until they look around.

A few replaced over a handful of days
maybe required to get the job done at all.

To make renovations, it took patience,
but it's worth the cost and look for attractiveness.

Thoughts Through Art

Individuals think through remarks made
about weather, nature, people, and politics.
News agencies present stories daily;
some are real-life tales while others they make up.
Poems are expressions of people's thoughts.

Persons want validation for exertion,
whether earning money for a career or art.
Being supportive helps others with confidence
which causes them to produce valuable items.
Society benefits from rustic objects.

The mind darts from one thing to another,
pondering things concerning people or events.
Coming up with words or ideas keeps people
from getting into others' business or evil things.
By keeping people busy, humans are functional.

Patricia Cruzan

A Person's Emotions Alter

In a moment, laughter changes
to a dam, letting go of tears.
Droplets become an ocean,
then dissipate as our fears.

Feelings of loneliness appear,
but friends enliven the soul
so that we strive to help others,
and kindness becomes our goal.

Terror grips one's reasoning
like fish breaking free from whales.
Their escape helps life go on,
giving them momentum like sails.

Anger now and then arises,
a tornado with much rain;
calmness returns to a soul
as a person leaves their pain.

An ENT Visit

A sinus infection continued for days
with nothing relieving the problem suffered.
A test request followed, and I reasoned the news
might be fair or hard to cope with right now.
The day for the test finally arrived,
and I traveled to Emory for the study.

Technicians treated me professionally and friendly,
and my fears settled about the assessment.
The ear tumor news didn't sound harmful
until hearing it touched the brain stem, too.
Magnetic resonance imaging followed
until information about the treatment.

I received radiation for days,
but after X-rays, the tumor
grew. A surgeon discussed removal
and planned my tumor date for surgery.
The doctor said, *My prognosis looked excellent.*
Years passed before the last healing came.

The Wait

Unhappy humans with blank stares
wait their fate in the waiting room,
remaining until they hear their name.

Most patients sit watching TV
while the announcer gives plenty of reports;
the patients listen for entertainment.

Talks go back and forth between the patients sitting
as they watch the clock in the waiting room
until one hears his name to go back to their room.

The sick one sees the examinable table
before getting on it with a stool
to recline on the narrow therapy space.

The person with the growth lies down quietly,
and a mask comes down on the patient's face
as a technician adjusts it for treatment.

Countless employees vanish during therapy
while the hum and drum begin throughout treatment,
and fractured beams flow to the tumor.

The radiation continues for minutes
and the patient's eyes close during delivery,
blotting out light beams that stop the tumor.

A ping resounds, then passes until
the therapy ends. The patient is happy
with steps in the distance, signaling release.

The mask comes off, and air rushes in
as the patient is free to pursue dreams
and satisfy requirements for comfort.

The Unexpected News

Constant emails arrive from the church weekly,
announcing surgeries, members' illnesses, and deaths.
Over a few days, updates
come in, and the papers give additions.

Members' news arrive in each inbox.
Many times, the relatives' names are unknown.
Today, the member's death caught me by surprise.
I sympathize with the family's suffering.

Questions start about the family's feelings.
One wonders the death cause since the one wasn't old.
Even though a person's not close to the kin,
thoughts about the family's needs enter a mind.

Prayer always helps because God knows the pain
and needs during this period after one's absence.
Relatives thrive on knowing each person's care
with cards, flowers, and meals sent to their homes.

Patricia Cruzan

Our Country's Flag and Freedoms

Old Glory waves, creating a plain view
while displaying the red, white, and blue.

The flag, a symbol, sways in the wind,
standing for freedom; we mustn't rescind.

It waves in the breeze without a crease.
We see it swing high in times of peace.

The flag flies half-mast for people aghast
for soldiers and others part of our past.

When leaders held meetings miles away;
 they faced debates and had their say.

Men have freedoms in the Bill of Rights
to keep people safe while facing their plights.

Leaders have protections from flawed laws,
and the constitution has few flaws.

People aren't fearful of what they believe;
subjects' beliefs, others can take or leave.

As a nation, we choose civil things to do.
We can attend church and sit in a pew.

The Appeal of the Sea

Looking at waves, like a kaleidoscope,
people wonder if rainbows' reflections
give hues or if algae alter the sea's tint.

Does the sun's mirroring through clouds cause streaks,
or do the sun's hues reflect on the waves,
falling through the air like a shining agent?

An ocean is sable as darkness descends,
preventing a person's vision of what's below,
but humans delight in echoing swells.

Outside Sights and Sounds

A bird song calls to me,
trilling a joyous note;
it sings a lovely tune,
and I rise with a jolt.

I listen to Father God
while strolling in the brush.
My dog inhales the scents
as I walk and don't rush.

My canine stops for food;
every tree it'll scour
before I pull it away
to not eat every hour.

Cheep sounds stop the hunter
in its ferocious search
for new morsels to eat
while it heads to the birch.

My dog goes on the path
until I change the route,
so we end up going home,
and the canine turns its snout.

The Brave Helping Others

Rushing in the location
presented dreadful conditions.
The firefighters and nurses
attended the fallen skillfully.

People gave up lives
as they bandaged wounds and tried
to help others. Fires flared
as firefighters fought.

Years later, brave people
appeared to save lives again.
What was in fearless minds
while paying the ultimate price?

People wanted to escape
while others offered their help
to those in hopeless positions.
Heroic efforts saved lives.

Considerate Deeds

Swiftly, utter kind words
to one who needs words of cheer.
When one struggles to speak,
lend a listening ear.

Generous words encourage
one who's fighting a disease.
Caring deeds meet the needs
of folks in a state of unease.

Relating to a person
means you communicate
while showing cogent thinking
you can accommodate.

Happiness for Others

To make one happy, we'll extend
the time a human has for fun.
At times it requires a person to bend,
but love demands moments, so don't run.

A person can plan scores of things.
One proposes how to show love now.
Can a human make others feel like kings,
or can one help with a special vow?

By the day's end, what have we sent out?
Did we check on one more human being?
Have we helped those with a positive doubt,
or did we assist a soul from fleeing?

Patricia Cruzan

Different Food at Mealtime

Getting in a rut isn't difficult
with the same kinds of food tempting,
but a few changes can result
in having health-giving dishes.

Too many provisions at one time
make it taxing to remember,
and throwing out food is a crime,
so one buys less at a store.

Meat often will taste first-rate
and give the protein we require.
The number of sweets from the plate
controls pounds people put on.

Eating from many food classes
isn't like we learned in school,
but vitamin C causes rashes,
so people want a food array.

Words Heard

I heard the words, *Oh, crap.*
Luckily, the language wasn't worse.
Happiness filled my soul
when no injury occurred climbing
up two steps on the ladder.

The scarf and curtain came down
for cleaning without more words.
With chemicals, the window grew
spotless and shined like new.
An owner treasured the work
performed. After drying curtains,
they looked pristine again.

Misapplication of Patience

Henry W. Longfellow said,
Let us then, be up and doing,
with a heart for any fate;
still achieving, still pursuing,
learn to labor and to wait.

We could rise early each day
and ascend before recharging.
We might get lots done at once
while tiptoeing as a sneak
and suffer from an energy crunch.

Often, life visions are lost
in our effort to get things done,
and we might stand by and wait
with ideas by the ton
until facing a chance fate.

Pluses of Staying Inside More

If the hair's wild, it goes unnoticed:
a strand may stick up slept on wrong.
If hair grows longer, groups miss it
unless you go on Zoom for a meeting.

Shaves are farther in-between
because inside, people don't see you.
Long times not shopping for critical items
make you invisible to kin and others.

Projects put on hold get done faster,
such as home sections not cleaned weekly.
Many tasks to do are time-consuming,
but they get our undivided attention.

Finding time to write is often a problem,
but noticeable soiled areas need cleaning now.
We have more time to complete the work.
Jobs are simple to do when time is there.

Making Bread for the First Time

Steps of letting the dough rise
didn't seem overwhelming,
but I didn't know how time flies
when trying to follow all steps.

Cooking takes concentration
as one gets the dough to rise,
and cooks want a foundation
so the consistency's right.

The portions must go in right
and put in to set and rise,
or you'll have a cooking blight
and it may cause you to sigh.

With attention to the mixture
and reading directions more times,
you'll be able to endure,
and your bread will be a success.

Cookies for a Family Christmas Party

Sugar cookies sounded like a treat
but they were a demanding feat.
My son liked them as a child
with his chosen flavor and style.

Portions and directions seemed easy,
and the order seemed like a teensy
bit of this and that with flour
and not many bowls to scour.

Adding right parts in order
made me like a brick toiler,
gathering tools for their trade
because I didn't have an aid.

All segments joined nicely,
and cookies weren't too spicy
as pieces clung together;
they weren't light as a feather.

Last, I added food dye,
but no amounts caused me to sigh
for having a perfect cookie
to serve as a goodie.

Love

Love: full devotion
to another
no matter the outcome

-

What Love Means

If we love someone,
we help them unselfishly
to bring happiness.
We give them moments daily
by going the extra mile.

Haiku and Senryu

ballet dancers
spinning tops
obscure outlines

yellow sunflowers
bumblebees
pleasing contrasts

a tiny white bird
cotton balls
springy

snow
an outer egg white
textures

deer whitetails
dogs rear appendages
shadowy waves

a snake coils
from a stove vent
pandemonium

shady path trees
scenic mountain trails
hiking in woods

songbirds
sopranos trill
notes reverberate

palm trees
handheld fans
Florida sun's respite

Patricia Cruzan

a windswept day
foamy waves
a shimmering sunrise

        a cassowary
        a crocodile
        giants

skiers
swimmers
over and under

        a dog's swishing tail
        a wolf wags its rear
        packs

a brake squeals
a barking retriever leaps
happy

        the newspaper's news
        out with yesterday's tabloids:
        the real truth

crows caw
a rabbit munches
vanish

        soup and salad
        a birthday meal
        two cake bites

fall's leaf piles
bare branches
arms naked

a waterfall
leaves
autumn

        real hounds
        art remembrances
        parts

the Louvre
the Giza Pyramid
towering edifices

        a tenor sax
        a Stradivarius violin
        euphony

woman of one hundred
tall rhododendron plants
age

        an angel
        a cloud-shaped messenger
        luminous

a castle over water
a skyward cross
rays

        a key chip
        dead battery
        locked car

insect feet
spiders' hooked claws
a web

wild beavers
dam designers
floods

        Gutenberg's printing press
        laptops and printers
        words

branches intermingle
two trunks
on opposite sides

        a beached starfish
        a large flower blooms
        attract

northern cardinals
scarlet robes
eye-catching

        a newspaper
        a radiation report
        current affairs

An Unforeseen Storm

Clouds of a sunless gray
appeared in midday.
The sky waxed jet black
no bright clouds were coming back.

The rain flecked vehicles
as drizzles came in trickles.
My auto looked slick,
and braking caused no click.

There came a booming sound
in the sky around;
the noise grabbed attention,
causing a pulse to quicken.

A steeple took a hit,
causing it to split.
The chapel had no one there,
but the din led to a scare.

Rainy Days

The silver-gray masses move in
from cumulonimbus clouds.
Sunny skies become smoky
against the powder-blue ether,
appearing as grayish skies.

Raincoats shield tourists,
acting as protective gear
while guests feel droplets to downpours
as they dash to cars from boutiques
while parasols protect.

Zippers help keep winds out
when heavens darken Earth,
and light crashes skyward
as clouds dispel torrents
while the welkin goes inky.

Storms Around

Showers drizzled for days,
and tornadoes hovered around.
People nervously watched
as storms came earthbound.

We prayed to God each day
for friends and kin living
close and farther away
who helped with Christmas giving.

People not known by us
lost homes and dress attire.
We don't know how they survived,
but they lost things in the mire.

Persons empathized,
but it's hard to feel one's pain.
We have houses to stay in
without fear of the rain.

Patricia Cruzan

The Weather People's Forecasts

A person smiles, predicting the cold.
Below freezing temperatures show for the zone.
We see twenty-nine predicted for the night,
so the thick comforter comes up for sleeping.
Flannel pajamas and slipper socks go on
to keep the body warm on toilet trips.

The blanket and sheet go around one's head,
keeping chilly air from creeping in the bed.
Adults make frequent turns for aching bodies.
Often, tissues shut out the noise all around.
We hope for fair conditions for eight hours,
and the bed's elevated for breathing.

—

The Temperature's Changing

Temperatures approach seventy degrees
when spring offers people longer days,
and many words come out with more ease,
because there's fresh energy from the sun's power.

The brightness supplies additional light
to view words better and to do that cleaning,
so people move faster without a flight.
We make haste before temperatures rise.

The Hot Weather Blues

Late at night, there always seems to be
one more show for concentration
before turning in for bedtime at night.

In the summer, the sun rises early.
Adults try to get up before nine,
checking emails and sites before writing.

If people wake early, they get up,
avoiding the heat to do physical work;
they labor before the heat builds up.

Avoiding heat can help humans rise
and have the energy for exertion,
so they can enjoy amusement later.

Patricia Cruzan

A Snowstorm in Early April

The day grew extremely cold,
but before, we had a warm day.
Snow appeared in the night,
and clouds turned to slate-gray.

The following day, people saw
flakes coating the ground,
and the dog rushed with full speed
to do business with a crunch sound.

It came right back inside
but left its tracks in the snow.
Afterward, we threw its ball,
and it chased the sphere to and fro.

While people completed tasks,
the dog found my husband's record.
It chewed the vintage album
because, with no chum, it got bored.

The retriever lived fifteen years;
album eating didn't kill it.
People never blamed themselves
for filling their years with rife.

A Missed Thunderstorm

The rains came late one night,
with first-rate sleeping conditions.
And thunder sent out such a light,
not like previous transitions.

With tissue shoved in an ear
and covers circling the neck,
I survived the night with no fear.
The house didn't change to a wreck.

The storm was highly severe,
shaking the house at least twice.
With logic, I had to revere
Christ spared us at any price.

Cinquains

summer
sultry, muggy
picnicking, sailing, frolicking
body temperatures climb up
July

-

vacation
enjoyable, pleasurable
traveling, boating, swimming
unstructured time for family
recreation

-

kindness
compassionate, considerate
assisting, serving, loving
not fearing others' actions
gentleness

-

unselfishness
humane, generous
freeing, giving, caring
aid provided when possible
devotion

Delighting in the Day

May the wind be at your back
while taking along your pack.
Enjoy the sunshine
along the coastline.

Each day take time for glances;
take time for life's dances.
Find pleasure in seeking laughter
and buying wares from a crafter.

Delight in your work and play,
and trust God as you pray
while helping along the way.
Then there's less chance to stray.

-

A Trip to the Beach

Waves wash on the shore,
pulling shells galore
while kids splash and ride floats
as teens paddle in boats.

Breakers knock seniors down
and cause them to frown.
They get help from strong men
to raise elders again.

All people want to have fun
in white caps in the sun.
A little time spent there
supplies one with fresh air.

The Author

Patricia Cruzan writes poetry and children's books: four poetry and seven children's books. Her poetry books are for adults, and the children's books are for ages six to sixteen. In less than a year, Patricia looks forward to having her first picture book published.

As a writer, she has poems in anthologies, stories, articles, and devotionals in various publications and websites. Her church and many libraries encouraged her to publish pieces.

Before writing, she taught in Georgia, Texas, and Louisiana. She taught high school music, elementary reading, and regular elementary grades until her retirement.